Spotlight on the
MAYA, AZTEC, and INCA CIVILIZATIONS

The Ancient INCA ECONOMY

Sarah Machajewski

PowerKiDS press™

New York

Published in 2017 by The Rosen Publishing Group, Inc.
29 East 21st Street, New York, NY 10010

Editor: Sarah Machajewski

Photo Credits: Cover, p. 11 Vadim Petrakov/Shutterstock.com; pp. 4,8 https://commons.wikimedia.org/wiki/File:Idiot_Empire.svg; p. 5 Y.a.r.o.m.i.r/Shutterstock.com; p. 7 DIANA NIKOLOVA/Moment Open/Getty Images; p. 9 https://commons.wikimedia.org/wikiFile:Pachacutec_statue,_Aguas_Calientes,_Peru.jpg; p. 10 DEA/G. DAGLI ORTI/De Agostini/Getty Images; p. 12 AIZAR RALDES/AFP/Getty Images; p. 13 Evans/Hulton Archive/Getty Images; p. 15 Westend61/Getty Images; pp. 16, 28 DEA/G. DAGLI ORTI/De Agostini Picture Library/Getty Images; p. 17 Diane Cook And Len Jenshel/National Geographic/Getty Images; p. 19 Jack Zalium/Flickr.com; p. 20 Jess Kraft/Shutterstock.com; p. 21 DEA / G. Dagli Orti/De Agostini/Getty Images; p. 22 Walter Pawlowski/Shutterstock.com; p. 23 Markus Daniel/Moment Open/Getty Images; p. 24 Arvind Balaraman/Shutterstock.com; p. 25 PavelSvoboda/Shutterstock.com; p. 27 Religious Images/UIG/Universal Images Group/Getty Images; p. 29 De Agostini/A. Dagli Orti/De Agostini Picture Library/Getty Images.

Library of Congress Cataloging-in-Publication Data

Names: Machajewski, Sarah, author.
Title: The ancient Inca economy / Sarah Machajewski.
Description: New York : PowerKids Press, 2017. | Series: Spotlight on the Maya, Aztec, and Inca civilizations | Includes index.
Identifiers: LCCN 2016000864| ISBN 9781499419382 (pbk.) | ISBN 9781499419412 (library bound) | ISBN 9781499419399 (6 pack)
Subjects: LCSH: Incas--Economic conditions. | Indians of South America--Peru--Economic aspects.
Classification: LCC F3429.3.E2 M33 2017 | DDC 985/.019--dc23
LC record available at http://lccn.loc.gov/2016000864

CPSIA Compliance Information: Batch #BS16PK: For further information contact Rosen Publishing, New York, New York at 1-800-237-9932.

CONTENTS

MYSTERIOUS MACHU PICCHU

A deserted city stands in the Andes Mountains in Peru. Ruins of homes, farms, roads, and **terraces** seem to blend in with the peaks and valleys of the surrounding landscape. This ancient city is Machu Picchu, and its builders were the Inca people.

The Inca people once ruled a great empire that spread across the present-day countries of Peru, Ecuador, Chile, Bolivia, Argentina, and Colombia, covering nearly 2,500 miles (4,023 km) from north to south. At its height, the population of the Inca Empire is estimated to have been around 12 million people.

The Inca civilization grew through the careful management of its land and **resources**. This created a successful and highly organized economy. However, the Inca people didn't use money. In fact, their society didn't even have it. Let's explore the Inca civilization and the way its economy worked.

Machu Picchu was just one of the Inca people's great achievements. The Inca economy would've influenced life here, just as it did in all Inca settlements.

THE INCA EMERGE

The Inca Empire ruled in the Andean region during the 15th and 16th centuries. However, **ancestors** of Peru's native people lived in the area thousands of years before that. The earliest settlements in the Sacred Valley, near present-day Cuzco, date back to about 4500 BC.

People of this time lived as hunter-gatherers, which means they hunted animals and gathered wild food to survive. Over thousands of years, they settled into villages. As these groups of people spread out and settled, they developed separate **cultures** and identities. The Inca people settled around the same time as the Aztecs, who were an important civilization in what is now present-day Mexico.

The first Incas probably emerged in present-day Peru during the 12th century. According to tradition, they lived about 15 miles (24 km) south of Cuzco in a village called Paqari-tampu. At some point between AD 1100 and AD 1200, they were led to Cuzco by their leader, Manco Capac. Cuzco became the Inca's permanent capital after that.

The Cuzco region contained several settlements belonging to people from different backgrounds. The Incas were just one, but they eventually became the most powerful.

THE RISE OF AN EMPIRE

The Inca's rise to power happened very quickly. When they arrived in Cuzco, the Incas forced the people already living there off their land.

The Inca began expanding in the 14th century under their fourth ruler, Mayta Capac. The Inca expanded their empire by **raiding** and looting neighboring villages. These people were allowed to remain free so long as they paid **tribute** to their conquerors.

Pachacuti Inca Yupanqui became the ninth **Sapa Inca** in 1438. During his reign, the Inca Empire slowly spread beyond the Sacred Valley. The Incas made their conquests permanent by keeping a military presence in the settlements they took over. Under Pachacuti, the Inca civilization became an empire they called Tawantinsuyu. In time, the empire would extend from parts of present-day Ecuador and Colombia to Chile and into Argentina.

Under Pachacuti, the Inca civilization became a well-organized empire with all the features of a developed society. This included a class structure, military, government, and economy.

WHAT'S AN ECONOMY?

An organized economy is necessary for a successful, strong civilization. An economy is the system that produces goods and services. Another part of an economy is how a society manages its resources. This means the economy determines the way the goods and services are used and given out.

A society's economy is important because it creates wealth, which gives a society power. Wealth can be measured in terms of money, but it also can be measured by how much a society produces and consumes.

In this 16th-century engraving, Inca farmers are shown planting corn. This kind of work was the backbone of the Inca economy.

The Inca didn't use money like we do, yet they had a very strong economy. It was based on other measurements of wealth, such as labor and agriculture.

In order to have an economy, a society must produce goods. There are three factors needed for production: land (and its resources), labor, and capital. Capital is everything, such as tools and production sites, needed to make goods or provide a service. The Inca Empire covered thousands of miles of land, ruled millions of citizens, and had capital to use. This helped establish a well-planned and strong economy.

THE EMPIRE GROWS

Pachacuti's military campaigns allowed the empire to expand, but the Incas didn't only conquer people by force. Sapa Incas sent representatives to settlements they wanted to join their empire. They offered valuable gifts to the settlements' rulers and offered to protect and manage their people. This **strategy** made the people in these settlements more accepting of the Inca's rule. Once these people joined the Incas, the government held the rulers' sons in Cuzco and educated them in the ways of the Inca.

QUECHUA MEN, 2010

The Inca conquered tribes of people who lived throughout the Andean region, including the Quechua people. The Quechua language was spoken throughout the Inca Empire.

QUECHUA WOMEN, 1955

In time, the Inca government gained a large amount of land. With it came a large population to manage. The Inca government became more organized as the empire grew, and it had a strong presence in people's daily lives. One way the Inca government cared for its people was through a centrally planned economy.

A BARTER SYSTEM

In a centrally planned economy, the government decides what's produced and how it's distributed, or handed out, to the people. The government manages the society's resources, including land and labor, and determines the best way to use them.

In the Inca society, the government provided for its people's basic needs. They had food, clothing, shelter, and tools—and they didn't need to buy any of this with money. If they needed something they didn't have, they could barter, or trade, for it.

Barter systems have been around for as long as societies have existed. In this kind of system, goods are exchanged for goods. In the vast Inca Empire, people living in one area specialized in producing certain goods, but may not have known how to make others. Bartering allowed people from all over the empire to have everything they needed.

Pictured here are the ruins of a village in the former Inca Empire. People of the village could barter with their neighbors, but the government provided for the people's basic needs.

AYLLU ECONOMICS

In order to understand how the Inca economy worked, it's important to understand how the society was organized. The Sapa Inca ruled from Cuzco, the capital. A governing body helped him make decisions. The rulers appointed administrators to supervise communities that were called ayllus.

16TH-CENTURY ENGRAVING OF CUZCO

Each ayllu was like its own tiny economic center. Each one had a role in creating the goods people in the Inca Empire needed to survive.

Ayllus are often described as networks of family groups that lived in the same area. They were **unique** to cultures from the Andean region of South America. Ayllus existed long before the Incas rose to power, but the Inca government transformed the ayllus into centers of economic productivity.

The Inca government owned the land occupied by ayllus. Administrators **assessed** the land and evenly distributed it among households in the ayllu. They also determined what the ayllu could do for the empire. Each ayllu was responsible for something different. Some specialized in growing crops, while others might have produced clothing. The government distributed these goods to other ayllus around the empire.

MIT'A LABOR

The success of an ayllu depended on all its citizens working together toward a common goal. This is called collective labor, and it was a driving force in creating the Inca's wealthy economy.

Married adult men living in the Inca Empire (including those from the nearly 100 nations conquered by the Inca) didn't just work because they wanted to—they worked because they *had* to. Citizens were required to pay a tribute to the government in exchange for what the government provided. However, they didn't pay with money—they paid with their labor. This tribute was required in addition to the farming each citizen had to do for the empire.

Laborers had to work for a certain amount of time during the year. When their service was over, someone else from the ayllu took over. This rotational service was called *mit'a*, which means "rotation" in the Quechua language.

The Inca Empire had no formal writing system, so record keepers kept track of *mit'a* labor, transactions, and taxes using quipus. A quipu was made of knotted cords hanging from a string. The colors, types of knots, and their placement on the string had special meaning for accountants.

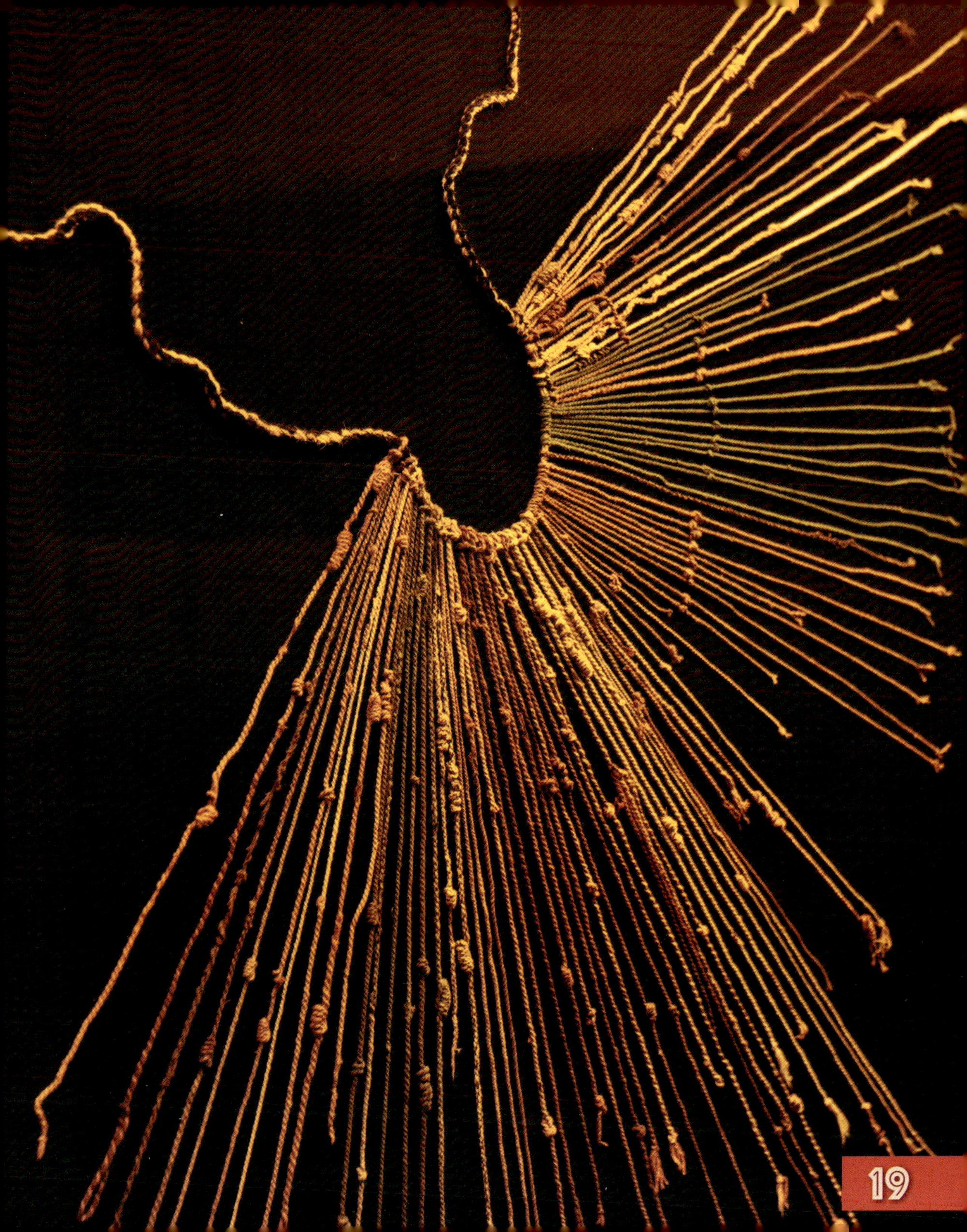

BUILDING AN EMPIRE

Mit'a laborers performed many kinds of jobs. They could be farmers, fishermen, messengers, miners, or builders. Some men were ordered to leave the ayllu to serve in the Inca army. Laborers performed tasks and worked on projects to improve the empire.

Mit'a labor gave the Inca Empire some of the features it's best known for—amazing buildings, structures, and roads. The Incas had one of the largest road systems of all ancient civilizations. It covered around 18,641 miles (30,000 km) and connected Cuzco to the most remote

The Inca Empire gained great wealth through *m'ita* labor. It allowed the Incas to build roads, cities, and structures, such as the baths pictured here.

reaches of the empire. Incas used the roads to transport goods between ayllus and for military or government projects.

The Inca people received food, tools, protection, and clothing from the government in return for their labor. Conquered territories received roads, monuments, and raw materials. This was called *ayni. Ayni* was a system of reciprocity, which means both sides received something in return for what they gave.

FARMING IN THE MOUNTAINS

The Incas had an economy based on agriculture. Food was the main good the society produced. Its large workforce allowed the Inca Empire to provide food for its millions of citizens. However, farming was no easy task in the Andes Mountains. The land was rocky and steep, with few natural sources of water. The Andean people solved this problem through terrace farming and irrigation.

Terraces are large steps built on the side of a mountain. Building terraces creates flat land that is suitable for farming. Terraces were good for growing crops because they collected water, which helped during **droughts**.

FARMING TERRACES

Inca farmers kept one-third of the food they grew. One-third went to the Sapa Inca as a tax. The government stored the food in great storehouses called *qollqa*. The food was used during famines, or food shortages. This way, no one in the Inca society went hungry. The remaining third went to priests, who used the food in religious ceremonies.

Without terraces, rainwater runs away. Through *mit'a* labor, the Inca also built **aqueducts** to carry water to and from the terraces.

Inca farmers grew maize (corn), squash, tomatoes, peanuts, chili peppers, and quinoa, which is a seed. Civilizations in this area were the first to grow potatoes. Farmers raised the crops that grew best in their climate, then traded for food from different areas of the empire.

RAISING ANIMALS

While some Inca citizens specialized in farming, others cared for animals and livestock. They raised dogs, guinea pigs, ducks, alpacas, and llamas. Alpacas and llamas were very valuable to the Inca. Some historians say the Inca Empire's wealth can be measured by how many of these animals it owned. The largest herds of these animals lived in the Lake Titicaca region in southern Peru.

The Incas raised llamas and alpacas for meat and for their wool. The wool was used to make clothing, mattresses,

Inca **textiles** were known for their decorative patterns. This Peruvian blanket borrows from that tradition.

Llamas and alpacas have warm, thick coats that can be used to make clothing. There's more than enough wool to go around!

and blankets. Llamas were also used as transportation and for carrying goods.

The Incas prized llamas and alpacas above all other animals because their wool was used to make fancy cloth, which was a treasure in Inca society. Fine textiles were extremely valuable and were often presented as gifts. Using its labor force and its herds of animals, the Inca Empire produced the kind of wealth it valued.

FESTIVAL DAYS

The Inca civilization is fascinating because it had great wealth without having money. Its wealth is better measured in its labor force and the food and valuable goods its citizens lived to produce. Though the citizens were forced to work by the empire, they were also rewarded.

Under the concept of *ayni*, the Inca government rewarded its people through festivals. During the festivals, the government provided large amounts of free food and *chicha*, which is a drink much like beer. These festivals lasted for several days. This put a stop to the labor that kept the empire going. However, these festivals made the Inca people more loyal to their rulers and created a deeper bond between them. Most importantly for the Inca rulers, the festivals may have made the Inca people more willing to accept their labor requirement.

Because of the kind of economy it had, some historians describe the Inca civilization as a "welfare state." A welfare state is a system in which the government provides for its citizens' needs.

THE FALL OF THE EMPIRE

The Inca society was one of the most powerful civilizations of the ancient world. Through territory conquests and a labor-driven economy, the civilization became extremely wealthy. Cuzco was the richest city in South America, containing stores of fine goods and metals, including gold. Tales of the empire's gold drew the Spanish to Inca lands.

Francisco Pizarro and a band of **conquistadors** first arrived in South America in the 1520s. Pizarro then left and returned in 1531 or 1532. In 1532, Pizarro and his crew captured the Inca emperor and marched to Cuzco to take its gold.

FRANCISCO PIZARRO

The Inca's forces were no match for the Spanish and their guns and modern weapons.

When they arrived, they couldn't believe the **opulent** wealth the city displayed. Pizarro and his men conquered the Inca relatively quickly. They defeated them in battles and squashed rebellions when they occurred. Many Incas died from sicknesses the Spanish brought with them from Europe. By 1572, the Spanish had complete control. After more than a century of power, the Inca Empire was no more.

THE SECRET CITY

The Spanish easily defeated the Incas and took over their land, except for one important settlement: Machu Picchu. Built in the 15th century, this city may have been a private residence for Pachacuti. It may have been a place for priests and other sacred people. Because the Spanish never knew about Machu Picchu, they didn't have the opportunity to take its goods or change it in any way. When it was discovered in 1911, it was clear it had been preserved more than any other Inca site.

Machu Picchu is one of the world's most important archaeological sites. It's taught us a lot about what the Inca Empire was like at the height of its power. It also displays important features of Inca society, such as terrace farms, architecture, and roads. While it's not certain what role this settlement played in the Inca economy, the economy most certainly had a hand in building it.

GLOSSARY

ancestor (AN-sehs-tuhr): Someone who comes before others in their family tree.

aqueduct (AH-kwuh-duhkt): A manmade channel used for carrying water.

assess (uh-SEHS): To measure the value of something.

conquistador (kahn-KEES-tuh-dohr): A Spanish conqueror of Mexico and Peru in the 16th century.

culture (KUHL-chur): The customs and ways of life of a society.

drought (DROWT): A long period of no rain.

opulent (AH-pyoo-luhnt): Displaying great wealth or riches.

raid (RAYD): A sudden attack on an enemy.

resource (REE-sohrs): A country's means of supporting itself, such as its land.

Sapa Inca (SAH-pah ING-kuh): An Inca ruler.

strategy (STRAA-tuh-jee): A plan of action for accomplishing something.

terrace (TAYR-uhs): A flat area cut into a slope, often to provide farmland.

textile (TEHK-styl): Cloth, or a fiber used to make cloth.

tribute (TRIH-byoot): An act, statement, or gift that is supposed to show respect or loyalty.

unique (yoo-NEEK): Belonging to one particular person or group.

INDEX

PRIMARY SOURCE LIST

Cover: Agricultural terraces at Moray. Created by citizens of the Inca Empire. Stone and earth. Pre-16th century. Located in southern Peru.

Page 10: Inca working in the fields. Created by Felipe Guaman Poma de Ayala. Published in *The First New Chronicle and Good Government*. Engraving. 1612–1615. Now kept in The Royal Library, Copenhagen, Denmark.

Page 15: Ruins of the village of Piquillacta. Built by the Wari people. Stone. ca. 1100. Located in southern Peru.

Page 19: Quipu. Created by unknown. Pre-16th century. Cotton or camelid fiber.

WEBSITES

Due to the changing nature of Internet links, PowerKids Press has developed an online list of websites related to the subject of this book. This site is updated regularly. Please use this link to access the list: www.powerkidslinks.com/soac/ince